W9-AUA-646

Universe War Five
The Supermyth

Omnipotence Era Exclusive
by
Caldwell Lee

Published by Caldwell Lee
CreateSpace.com

Copyright © 2011 by Caldwell Lee
All rights reserved
No part of this book may be reproduced in
any form without permission in writing
from the author.

ISBN 10: 1-45382-092-2
ISBN 13: 978-1-45382-092-6
LCCN: 2010916003

Printed in the United States of America
Createspace.com

Poetry reprinted from:
Meet the Poet: Aura of Love
The Forthright Omnipotence Era Series
ISBN 13: 978-1-45281-155-0
LCCN: 2010906722

Also by Caldwell Lee:
The Forthright Omnipotence Era Series
ISBN 978-1-45281-155-0
The Forthright Omnipotence Era Epic
ISBN 978-1-45054-129-9
The Forthright Omnipotence Era Relived
ISBN 978-1-59872-992-4
The Forthright Omnipotence Era
ISBN 978-0-80593-526-4

Createspace.com
An Amazon.com company

See also:
Instant Publishers.com
Dorrance Publishing
Barnes and Noble.com

Contents

Contents

Foreword
M.A.R.C.E.L.

Universe War Five ended in glory.
Many proclaimed it, the Supermyth
story.
From extraterrestrial celebrations to
the big city streets.
Global celebrations of those many
unimaginable accomplished feats.
In the end however, it would end in
disaster.
Did the Martians ultimately get what
they were initially after?
Or did other forces and entities come
into play?
No one had answered those questions to
this day.
Humans had never had anyone to act on
their behalf.
To locate and research the infamous
space craft.

Alas one day the Boy Superhero went prying.
Just no harm in a little research and trying.
At last he came upon the destroyed craft out in space alone.
He wanted to find something to secretly research on his own.
He found a little black box and knew he may have found his great need.
So he took it to the Powerplex, to where he could further proceed.
Powerplex computers opened a video ensemble of events.
From the persons aboard the shuttle to how the Supermyth came and went.
He saw a dark shuttle, then the Supermyth appear.
He saw a shuttle full of passengers panic from fear.
He saw the Supermyth crash into the shuttle and become powerless.
Then looks of succumb from all the rest.

Marcel said the Supermyth, it's the end of me.

It's not Marcel said a female voice, why couldn't any of us just see.

The two moons said the Supermyth, but before he could go on.

A thunderous clap and the shuttle was gone. Only a burnt out hull with no passengers in sight.

The dark destroyed shuttle in the dark of the night.

Another explosion, but no more visible picture.

The Boy Superhero just wasn't too sure. But he had to draw a conclusion and make some decisions.

Get a true definitive plan without revisions. The other heroes may catch on to him, so he had to act soon.

He had to figure out Marcel, the female's comments and the meaning of two moons.

Preface
M.A.R.C.U.S.

Powerplex computers did a decipher of
Marcel.
Boy Superhero deliberated, well, well, well.
Martian Android Robotic Control Entity
Link.
Boy Superhero began to think.
Martians of course, and the two moons of
Mars.
Boy Superhero took to the stars.
Llygentsheintshet on Mars began to explore
extensively.
Probably nothing in the open that he would
immediately see.
Whatever he needed to find was most likely
concealed.
His notion of acquiring knowledge felt
authentic and real.

Martian surveillance images of the boy
hero proclaimed it an addressable prank.
Martian ships fired upon the hero, hitting
him point blank.
It prompted the boy hero to destroy several
ships of a Martian fleet.
The Martian aggression became difficult to
defeat.
His research and investigation was about to
fail.
Not having enough time to examine the two
moons in detail.
He must subdue the remaining Martian
crafts and return at a later date.
Ruining his need to thoroughly investigate.

.

After ending the upheaval, the boy hero returned to his Earth home.
Sat at the Powerplex computers to ponder all alone.
Powerplex message flash, stating a day the for the Earth to regret.
The finding and destruction of boy hero, Llygentsheintshet!

This corresponds with a declaration of war on Earth and it's allies.
Soon Martian ships will take to the skies.
The Boy Superhero had a look of anxiety
The message was one, he didnt want the other heroes to see.

So he told Powerplex computers to go into scramble mode.

Any Martian message of sort was to deplete and erode.

Override any message in the solar system from reaching any Earth household.

Create a message to Earth computers that a Martian computer virus was to unfold.

Powerplex computers worked like a gem.

Martian declaration of war was depleted throughout the solar system.

Attack plan Marcus was put in motion by the Martians.

The heroes of the Earth not ready to defend.

The Martian Android Reality Control Unit Series.

While the Boy Superhero began to display his anxiety and worries.

Classic
Poetry

Stargistacola

The echoing sounds of shattering glass.
A bang , a pop, and then a blast.
She raced across the room, then out the
door.
Her precious little vehicle was to be no
more.
Across the street she went, a probable
suspect.
Returned with hands on hips, by her
notorious wreck.
Telephoning a friend, she caught a ride
across town.
Waited until the evening to sneak around.
Then gazing and drawing closer as if
under a hex.
Came upon a marvel of a structure,
called the Powerplex.

Quickly she jumped back, thought she'd
been heard.
Saw an image in the window, and
thought, this is absurd.
Contemplating drawing closer, then the
decisive, ah rats!
Stared into a window, eyes popping,
Keith Katz.
When he turned his back, entered another
room and did delay.
She sneaked through an open door and
hid away.
Exiting the building suddenly, the entire
system shut down.
Not an exit left open, not a light to be
found.
So in pitch black darkness, fearing to do
anymore than just kneel.
Was the darling young sweetheart, the
lovely Camille.

Pushing a sequence of buttons, all air
passages became blocked.
She became pale and blue, started to
wobble and rock.
Grabbing a small box, she proceeded to
the center of the room.
Pointed it to the ceiling, and directed it's
zoom.
Down came a partition, transparent and
clear.
Knocking her on the shoulder blade, her
head it did near.
Scrambling to a rollover, it came down
on her heel.
In agony and in pain, she began to
holler, cry, squeal.

Stargistacola

The partition wall bounced up, then came
down as before.
She looked squeamishly at the blood,
was queasy about the gore.
She rolled out of harm's way, collapsed,
staggered and fell.
Of such beauty and loveliness, for such
torment and hell.
The box device she had lost, began to pant,
suffocate.
Her life nearing the end, how bestowed
her this tragic fate.
Down came ceiling fragments, but she
had collapsed, fallen out.
It was Swytestar the superhero, a rescue
attempt, no doubt.

He gently cuddled her, then felt her head.
Took her pulse to be sure that she wasn't
dead.
Gave her mouth to mouth resuscitation,
which didn't revive her.
So he knelt to her side, to keep his head
clear.
Taking her to another room, he prepared
her to convey.
Gave her a kiss on the cheek and they
were on their way.
Later the next night, she was seen by
Powergent.
The great Dr. Josephson, to whom so
much this beauty meant.

Stargistacola

He performed surgery, using the extent of
his planet's data and cures.
Administered in such a way, in that super
powers it assures.
So presently, like all of nature's finest, in
the open air and carefree.
Like a bird, a bee, a flower, a tree.
She's now a female hero, a heroine.
She's the utmost, the dazzling, the most
famous, the end.
So now called Stargistacola, by her male
friends.
Her old fears are now gone, her new life
begins.
And like her foregone trials and
tribulations, where against her no man
can win.
The war has started so let the battle
begin!

The Time Being

Landing on the moon, on his return trip to Earth.
Swytestar gathered possessions, citing valueless worth.
For whom once these belongings were, no longer had inference.
And like the countless lost memoirs, it just didn't make sense.
Bye-bye, he said lowly, then suddenly, what was he seeing.
Then instantaneously gripped in the clutches of the Time Being.
The Time Being was listless, hard, cold and strong.
Of superhuman strength, used to do only harm.

The Time Being

The beings were numerous, the hero they
were to smash.
Their bodies were impervious, they were
as quick as a flash.
Descendants of Agod, where from the
exploding sun.
Is where their revived and vigor strength
had totally come.
Humans left for dead with their thought
control in tact
Then their backbones snake infested, to
life, they were brought back.
Snakes from the exploding sun to whom
Agod was once great.
Now the Time Being is the product, for
those who desecrate.

But Swytestar was no slouch, perhaps the
greatest hero that ever lived.
Ready for as much hell as they could
possibly give.
The Time Being he had shaken, he had
relinquished too soon.
Two others he tossed from the surface of
the moon.
Three more he smeared, let out highly
shriek cries.
But the most shocking to Swytestar, is
that , they all turned to flies.
Swytestar activated the starcar computers
to give the absence a brief.
The hero then hovered in outer space in
total disbelief.

All alone in a bed, between midnight and
noon.
Lies a beautiful young lady, singing a
beautiful tune.
Powergent, Powergent, I need you right
now.
Come to me please, someway, somehow.
She closed her eyes for a brief moment.
And opened them upon the arrival--
Powergent.
Wow she said, what a hunk of a man.
Stay all night, if you wish, if you can.
Then he looked into her eyes, shined his
pearly whites.
And said beautiful young ladies,
shouldn't have lonely nights.

Powergent

Your night will be enjoyable, and one well
spent.
Just repeat to yourself, I love you
Powergent.
Powergent, Powergent, from where
comes your name.
Power through the attainment of
knowledge and fame.
And gent by ladies whom have
challenged my best.
In games of faith, love, trust contests.
Ladies by whom on a mission I am sent.
To teach the art of love--Powergent.
Powergent, you're so charming and nice.
Someone I know needs your advice.
My younger brother, he studies not.
His mind is corrupt, his pants are hot.

Powergent

Sure said Powergent I will instruct the lad.
For my knowledge is thrice that of the
top college grad.
Powergent, Powergent, on what do you
thrive.
From where comes your strength, what
keeps you alive.
Love he said, is what will keep me
strong.
Without it my strength and powers and
gone.

Universe War Five

The Supermyth

28
Boy Superhero Quote

29
Supermyth Photo

The Supermyth, said the Boy Superhero of Universe War Five.

I often wonder, if he's still alive!

Universe War Five

The Supermyth

The Supermyth

My home is here, he said in a gentle
voice.
To a globally televised applause of
rejoice.
He was Babbles Lecastle, superb teenage
mind.
The most brilliant and decorated human
of his time.
From his telescopes at home he was a
star gazer.
In the rocket ships he built, he was a star
chaser.
Often times he'd leave without a trace.
To seek asteroids and meteorites in
outer space.
Effin Babbles Lecastle was his name.
Exploring moving objects in outer space
was his claim to fame.
He loved Earth's moon as a getaway.
Put a telescope there and there he would
stay.

The Supermyth

While observing one day from his
telescope tower.
He noticed a sensational meteor shower.
Took no messages and had no messages
sent.
In his rocket ship and off he went.
He landed his ship on the Ganymede
moon.
 Anxious to observe, he acted real soon.
He disabled his craft to be alone.
No possible communications from his
Earth home.
Years passed by the former young teen
gone without a trace.
People of the Earth declared Babbles
dead in space.

Before repairing his ship, he noticed from afar.
A dying, weakening, falling star.
From the constellation Aquila, it was Altair.
He had very little time to get out of there.
Leaving the Ganymede moon was his most urgent notion.
Upon liftoff there was an enormous explosion.
The once brilliant boy teen in a super nova collision.
Merely out on a star chasing, meteor shower mission.
Ironic indeed was his demise.
Researching and studying amongst the stars and the skies.

Dust particles from the super nova covered his space craft.

Communications with the Earth were no longer left.

On Earth the final decision was reluctantly given.

Babbles Lecastle was now definetly no longer living.

Within the covered dusty space craft the computers flashed and blinked.

Into the Super nova dust the body of Babbles continued to sink.

Once completely covered, the body began to rise.

The sensational young wonder opened his eyes.

Survival mode of the computers in tandem
with the super nova dust.
Had created a being of superb strength and
awesome lust.
He raised his arms wide, stretched
out and began to cry.
Happy as hell, that he did not die.
Flexed his knees to jump, and not
only jump high.
Babbles Lecastle began to fly.
His space craft only junk, nothing of
visible worth.
Left him with only one means of
returning to Earth.
But was he only dreaming, could he
really fly.
Nothing else to do, but actually try.

He took to flight time and time again.
He'd go a short distance, then take a
 longer spin.
Flight seemed possible but what about
 his strength.
Needed something to test it, he'd go to
any length.
So he put his hands firmly on his space
craft.
Started to giggle a lot, and let out a
laugh.
Thinking, If I can do this, I'll probably
never die.
Wishful thinking, but let's give it a try.
 The space craft moved with ease and
was soon above his head.
Looks like Babbles Lecastle will never
 be dead.

He also noticed that before giving the
craft a fling.
He did not want it to hit or hurt
anything.
He was in love with all life, that he
did know.
He was becoming a real life, actual
superhero.
So he separated his shuttle into pieces
and dispersed it into space.
Launching several pieces to the stars,
gone without a trace.
Babbles Lecastle, now flying through
space on his own.
Finally heading back to Earth, alone
towards home.

When he returned to Earth, a lot didn't
make sense.
He wanted to tell everyone of his
experience.
Technology itself had greatly increased.
And the hustle and bustle of life had
greatly decreased.
He wanted to tell of his powers, his
eyes did glisten.
No one however, no one would listen.
Everyone and anyone became his aim
to avoid.
They seemed too bland like that of a
robot or android.
So he headed to the place of his home
so dear.
For safe haven, rest, and to do research on
his computers there.

Once at home, on the computers he
logged on.
Something however seemed terribly
wrong.
His name Babbles was false and untrue.
He must log on as McCalsa Televu.
McCalsa Televu, he did not know.
In order to find him, where must he go.
He asked the computer, the answer
not very far.
Simply go to a room, in your
hideaway cellar.
He went below ground to his safe
haven cellar.
A body wrapped in a blanket simply
lay there.

He walked towards the body and pulled
the blanket off.
A female laying there began to noisily
cough.
He touched her, shaking her and said
Babbles is my name.
She said, your life is in danger, please
go away, just the same.
I'm Babbles, he said this is my home, who
are you.
She said, Babbles is dead stranger, I need
McCalsa Televu.
That's it he said, that's what my
computers say.
Can you please answer me, in a
sensible way.
She said you're one of them from the UFO.
Please don't touch me, please let me go.

See that she said, do you hear that
sound.
Either way, your over conversing has got us
found.
Every building, everywhere is under a
spy eye.
They're coming in for us, we are
going to die.
He stood up , turned around with
blanket in his hand.
Creatures came towards him, and
said come with us human.
They came towards him, he said, I
don't think so.
One said take the female, Babbles
said , let her go.

The Supermyth

The lead creature walked towards him,
put a hand on his shouder.
Said you my dear friend, couldn't be
any bolder.
So the creature took the blanket and it
draped on Babbles shoulders.
The creature said you my friend will
always look bolder.
So he called to another creature, and
said come here attach this thing.
The bold one here, will be the Earth king.
The lady began to scream loud, fainted
after a crying shout.
Just then came and array of ballistics
and shots rang out.
Earth's tactical team from behind the walls.
A piercing scream would be their attack
call.

Earth's tactical team came in on the
creatures.
The lady very motionless, just lay there.
Earth's tactical team was no match for
the creatures arsenal.
The entire tactical team began to fall.
When the last tactical team member had
finally fallen.
The creature pointed to the others and
said begin the Martian calling.
Not so fast said Babbles, what's going
on.
Ignore the human said the leader, we'll
take him along.

Babbles grew mad and stormed towards
the creature tandem.
Grabbed two of them at once and
proceeded to throw them.
Their powerful stun guns and lasers
left Babbles with a smile.
He simply stood there, cracking his
knuckles for a while.
When they got vicious, he resumed his
fight.
Showing every bit of his new found
might.
When he finished the creatures and they
all seemed dead.
He rushed over to lift the young lady's
head.

She suddenly awakened to a jump and a
scream.
Babbles said listen, you're in a dream.
She smiled, then said, you bet and alive.
Tell me dear Babbles, how did you
survive.
No , no he said, I'll listen to you.
Just continue to call me McCalsa Televu.
That's over she said, at least for now.
Every building has a spy eye, don't ask
me how.
She told him how the aliens had
conquered the Earth.
How no one's life had any worth.
Then once they selected a king for the
human race.
They'd contact the Martians to put final
rule in place.

The Supermyth

So that's why you screamed, he said
with a smile.
We'll have to stay here and plan for a
while.
She said out there, danger still looms.
And I didn't know you had powers, I
thought we were doomed.
But you didn't know me he said, and I
didn't know you.
And you and the computers are calling me
McCalsa Televu.
I did that she said when the aliens first
got here.
Everyone began to flee, full of fear.
So I came to the place of my long lost
lover.
Locked the doors and watched the alien
crafts hover.

The Supermyth

Earth's tactical team, said please beware.
We're behind your walls, just don't get
captured out there.
The aliens would learn from absorbing
one's personal identity.
They'd absorb the knowledge and let the
indiviual be.
So knowing how brilliant you were,
Babbles my dear.
I told a tactical team and we all just
stayed here.
I remembered a name from our childhood
life.
A name we used, when playing doctor
and wife.
I'd wished you'd remember, really I do.
Dr. and Mrs. McCalsa Televu.

The Supermyth

Babbles she said, darling we really
have trouble.
We'd better come up with a plan, on
the double.
One thing he said, what's with laying
in the cellar.
Ah aliens she said, like they're
everywhere.
When I thought they were closing in
she said, I'd run downstairs.
Lay there with eyes shut to fight off my
fears.
It would give team tactical time to fight.
Ready their munitions and get the aliens in
their sight.
Then I'd think of our childhood, me and
 you.
Said help me my darling Dr. Televu.
All I could think of was me and you.
Mr. and Mrs. McCalsa Televu.

She the took the blanket from Babble's
shoulders and stared in his eyes.
Let me help you Babble's give the
world a surprise.
She took the blanket from his strong
shoulders and held it in her hand.
Told him that she was ready to help
him plan.
She told him she'd design him a lovely
new cape.
She informed him of how the alien
mission was to take shape.
She told him the aliens had a specific
location to congregate.
How the Martians would eventually
come to help seal their fate.

The Supermyth

How alien ships would conquer an area
and leave their space ship stationed.
Then a Mothership would take the
aliens to their specific location.
Leaving areas of silly, simple humans
around enormous space crafts.
Babbles in all seriousness, just had to
laugh.
He gathered himself and began to
listen again.
Letting all she was telling him to
thoroughly sink in.
Then she said Babbles, let me break
off.
Choked a little, then a little cough.

Babbles she said, before all of this started.
After you'd gone and long departed.
I'd become confused and lost my way.
I'd plan to marry a new boyfriend
fiance'.
I see said Babbles, so how does this fit
in.
He was zapped by aliens, I want him
normal again.
I see said Babbles, then what from
there.
I don't know she said, I'm so full of
fear.
They looked at each other and began
to embrace.
Babbles then proceeded to wipe the
tears from her face.

Putting their personal concerns aside, they
began fresh and new.
Time was of the essence of what next to
do.
After discussion and research, their
answers were more than mere illusion.
They had a hard, decisive, and a workable
conclusion.
The control of the human thought was
based on the formation of alien ships.
Destroy the formation and break the
thought grip.
Destroy the vessels entirely would
restore human common sense.
Eliminate the Mothership and bring
back human intelligence.

The Supermyth

He logged on to his computer to visibly
view the Earth from it.
While she at other computers created
an impervious cape and outfit.
Her job was to analyze the aliens from
the computers without fear.
Once he started his assault to get the aliens
out of there.
To remove the aliens from Earth once
and for all.
Before they had a chance to make the
conclusive devastating Martian call.
Babbles had to act fast, his childhood
sweetheart and lover in place.
And then he set off to save the entire human
race.
Historians tout Universe War One as no
picnic.
Many have proclaimed it not bearable
and sick.

The Supermyth

The human race virtually conquered with
no one or nothing to intervene.
Then an unlikely young myth of a hero
returns to the scene.
Only assisted by his once beautiful
young lover.
While space ships abundant, land and
hover.
This is the stuff fairy tales are made of.
Now it's in the true life of Babbles and
his love.
But Babbles Lecastle was up for the task.
Persons of that era just love to be asked.
They tell of how Babbles started late into
the night.
Destroying alien ships to even the fight.
Bringing back common sense and human
thought.
How Babbles the Supermyth tactically
fought.

The Supermyth

How the alien creatures became dastardly
mean.
While seeing their many space crafts
smashed to smithereens.
The aliens still hopeful, brought on the
Mothership.
Babbles destroying it broke all of the
thought grip.
He was Babbles Lecastle, a legend, the
Supermyth.
But who were the Earth people, that he
was now with.
So he called of his lover, his long time
girlfriend.
And asked of her secrecy of who he was
and where he'd been.
Even returned to normal, Earth people
were simply human.
He just knew in his mind that they
wouldn't understand.

The Supermyth

So end Babbles Lecastle, bring on
McCalsa Televu.
I'm the Supermyth he said, what can I
do for you.
She looked at him smiled, and kissed
his lips.
Stood there delicately with hands on her
hips.
She said , well there superhero get on
your knees.
Isn't it time, you proposed to me.
He looked at her with concern, really me
and you.
Mr and Mrs. McCalsa Televu.
That's right she said, exactly how it
seems.
My husband, my Supermyth, the man of
my dreams!

The Supermyth

After getting married, Babbles asked of
her other friend.
She said, she had seen him around
every now and then.
Babbles asked her to stay friends with
the other guy.
Even ask him over, try not to ask why.
So she asked her friend over and when
he came through the door.
Babbles Lecastle fell to the floor.
McCalsa she said , something's gone
wrong.
Help me she said, what is going on.
She ran towards the phone yelling,
help me please.
Her boy friend of old got to his knees.
He knelt beside the body and said look
at you.
The man who took my woman,
McCalsa Televu.

He searched the body of McCalsa and
when he did.
He found a wallet somewhat well hid.
He stared in the wallet and said Effin
Babbles Lecastle, what is this.
She screamed over towards him,
stomping and raising her fists.
Effin Babbles Lecastle, I know you.
What's all this McCalsa Televu.
I hate you she said, and that's a
fact.
I'm leaving he said, and I won't be
back.
Once he was out the door , she wiped the
 tears from her eyes.
Babbles Lecastle began to rise.
What happened he said, where did
your friend go.
I told him to leave, I just didn't
know.

The Supermyth

I wanted to speak with him, but I was
caught off guard.
Get him back here, stall him in the
front yard.
I want to examine him thoroughly a
little more distant.
Something about him, knocked me
out in an instant.
Beg him to come back, in me place
your trust.
Promise to have sex, do what you
must.
When her friend returned, she got him
to get nude.
She looked at him and said, I'm not
trying to be rude.
But your clothes are dirty and of an
awful smell.
I'll take them downstairs and wash
them well.

The Supermyth

She ran downstairs where Babbles was
waiting.
A scanning process he was creating.
After scanning the clothes Babbles gave
up and said no.
What's going on, where must I go.
As he debated and rolled his fingers.
Once again the weakness began to linger.
At the top of the stairway was their half
naked friend.
Shut the door said Babbles, don't let him
in.
As she closed the door Babbles said,
there is something you must get.
On his right arm. I need that bracelet.
Put it in this container, before you bring
it down.
Do not let that guy leave these grounds.

The Supermyth

Once getting the bracelet, Babbles had it
analyzed.
The once powerful Babbles with tears in
his eyes.
Get your friend said Babbles, now we
really need to talk.
Her friend looked frightened, almost
afraid to walk.
Where did you get this, Babbles did ask.
Hurry up and talk, please talk man fast.
I got it from the aliens, at the signing of
peace treaty.
They only handed out one, so I couldn't
get greedy.
This bracelet is made from particles of
the super nova dust.
It must always stay concealed, that is a
must.

And second of all, for a gift it's not nice.
For it's also contains a tracking device.
What said their friend, too fast let's go slow.
She filled their friend in so he could understand and follow.
Now said Babbles, the real reason I wanted you here.
Pay close attention, keep your head clear.
We need to be close friends, be always by our side.
Some one in which we can always confide.
We in return will be your best friends.
Never ever should you have a problem again.
The one job you will have, the job all your life.
The secrecy between, me you and my wife.

The Supermyth

People will always need help, where to
turn, where to go.
This is your job, for you will know.
When danger comes and trouble looms.
When an alert needs to be sent to stop
the inevitable doom.
They will want the Supermyth, without
hesitation.
Just give them the Supermyth without
frustration.
Just say , yeah the Supermyth, I know
what to do.
Just contact his bosom buddy, McCalsa
Televu.
So the three best friends, put any
differences aside.
Ready to take heroism totally in stride.
Many believed that they actually had fun.
Preparing for the future after Universe
War One.

The Supermyth

64

Other Universe Wars came to the Earth
planet.
Humans with the Supermyth didn't
worry a bit.
Universe Wars Two and Three the Earth
reigned in glory.
But Universe War Four was a different
story.
Aliens returned with a small Martian
contingent.
And the million dollar question was
where the bracelet went.
Martian in the company of humans and
aliens.
Disguised themselves as very close
friends.

The Supermyth

When they disguised themselves as
McCalsa's wife's other friend.
She opened the door and let them in.
When the actual friend came by, he
stayed calm and poised.
Even with what he saw after hearing
cellar noise.
A likeness of him, so exact and perfect.
He picked up the phone, then put it
back.
So he sent a single distress signal to
the Supermyth.
Then waited and kept an eye on
whoever she was with.
When Supermyth arrived, the friend
had passed out from fret.
His wife he saved and hid but gone was
the bracelet.

He told the friend, not to worry at all.
Be firm, get up stand strong and tall.
He told him that he would take him to
alien ship.
Just hang in there and bite his lip.
The bracelet was missing, that could prove
disastrous.
Finding the bracelet was a definite must.
The tracking device was removed when
it was taken.
So it's impossible to trace and why are you
shaking.
The aliens, he said, they're standing
right over there.
Now they're proceeding to come right
over here.
The Supermyth flew up, said kill him
he's yours.
Then came the mysterious opening of
the alien ship doors.

The Supermyth

Then what of the girl, said the aliens
determine her fate.
Why not said the Supermyth, she's only
your duplicate.
The aliens grew mad, asked where is she.
My business said Supermyth, on first
distress, she was free.
Without another word, the alien ship was
smashed.
His friend scared to death went into a
mad dash.
Stood behind Supermyth, gagged and
coughed.
Said go on Supermyth, finish them off.
No said Supermyth, we'll let them be
be on their way.
You're not going to die, and neither are
they.

The Supermyth

The aliens heard him, said Supermyth
whatever you do.
Think about those words, as if they pertain
to only you.
You're vulnerable Supermyth, we will
be back, yes we will.
The legendary Supermyth, will be our
prize kill.
They boarded a ship, recently arrived.
It exited to the skies, then returned in a
dive.
Then they jettisoned off into the night
so black.
You're letting them go Supermyth, just
like that.
Yes said Supermyth, I called their bluff.
Ordinary alien invaders whom have had
enough.

When the Supermyth momentarily had
baited his friend.
He was searching for the bracelet the
aliens had taken.
Because his friend had fainted from
fear.
When Supermyth saved his wife, the
bracelet was not there.
He knew the aliens had it, the tracking was
gone or changed.
How it's many particles may have been
rearranged.
He knew that if they returned with a
chemical substance.
Not even he, the Supermyth could
stand a chance.
So he told his friends to always be on
guard.
One day the aliens might hold the
perpetual high card.

So begins the story of Universe War
Five.
The promise that no humans would
remain alive.
Initial detonations of air, space and
ground.
The legendary Supermyth, nowhere to
be found.
Precipitation had been heavy on a cold
cloud top day.
In the snowcap mountains, a group of
friends hideaway at play.
McCalsa and a group of friends on a
snow trip.
When came the whislting sound above
of UFO space ships.
Looking overhead, they could not
believe their eyes.
Multiple large spacecafts flooded
the skies.

Martians they said, as they all headed
for cover.
Frantically board their snowmobiles
while the large ships hover.
McCalsa told his friends, he was to
take a detour.
His friends all yelled what on Earth
for.
Soon McCalsa Televu had sped out of
sight.
His friends continued on full of fear
and fright.
He called to his wife's good friend,
told him to go stay with her.
He had some Martian ships to bring
down and then he'd be there.
Had Universe War Five had just begun.
Martians subdued before firing a shot, but
had the Earth won.

After conquering the first alien ships
there was a long pause and silence.
When he called his wife and friend,
they were nervous and tense.
They told McCalsa that no one was
safe to be with.
That Martians were on a mission to
bring down the Supermyth.
Newscasters were reporting that aliens
and villains had found.
A chemical agent that could bring the
Supermyth down.
McCalsa told them not to worry and
keep a smile on their faces.
He'd be there after taking captured
Martians to secure confined places.
Supermyth was confident as he hung
up the phone.
Then he sealed the captured Martians
and headed on home.

The Supermyth

When Supermyth got home, he began to
show worry.
Grabbed the television remote in a big
hurry.
He had a look of seriousness without
a smile.
None of his phone devices had rung
for a while.
But the most important thing of all
is that being at home.
There was no way in hell, that he
should be alone.
McCalsa grew angry , he remembered
their discussion.
Told his wife to go home and stay
with their good friend.
McCalsa sat down, thinking to act.
Arms spread across his sofa seat back.

Then a surprise when he turned the
television on.
Martian and alien ships were long
from gone.
People of the planet Earth were full of
fear.
Martians with their duplicating ability
were everywhere.
Emails flooded in, text messages went
beserk.
Persons interviewed on tv were
calling McCalsa a jerk.
Taking his mind off the attackers
for his beautiful wife to be with.
And not even getting in touch with
the Supermyth.

The Supermyth

The Supermyth sat there all alone.
Came an erratic voice, McCalsa man,
pick up the phone.
But Supermyth knew that danger was
present and clear.
And his beautiful wife wasn't even there.
Then the phone rang again, McCalsa
stared at the tv.
McCalsa said the message, McCalsa
listen to me.
McCalsa you're probably mad that
we didn't come there.
The Martians man, they are everywhere.
It's me said the voice completely out
of breath.
Your wife has been captured, they're
going to put her to death.
The've developed a chemical agent
to destroy you.
They're saying try to save your wife
to prove their theory true.

McCalsa just sat there, hands across the
sofa.
What on Earth was all of this for.
McCalsa then focused on the television
again.
Impersonating Martians were world
leaders and newsmen.
Then breaking news came, saying
McCalsa Televu.
The aliens have your wife, where are
you.
They don't really care what you do
or who you're with.
They simply want you to contact, the
Supermyth.
But McCalsa Televu, in his guise.
Could only sat and watch, with tears
in his eyes.

No one knows the real mood of McCalsa
Televu that day.
But he gathered himself enough to send
the Martians on their way.
Freed his wife and saved the world.
Preserved the love of his childhood
girl.
Effin Babbles Lecastle now McCalsa
Televu.
Ended Universe War Five with little
left to do.
Debated a shuttle mission to destroy
the deadly lethal chemical compound.
The once Effin Babbles Lecastle lost in
space and starbound.
The battle against Agod left him
never to be found.
His victory in Universe War Five,
left him legendary and reknowned.

Universe War Five

The Boy Superhero

The Boy Superhero

The Supermyth said the Boy Superhero
Of Universe War Five.
I often wonder, if he's still alive.
Constant Marcus Anselm,
Llygentsheintshet.
The Supermyth hero he had never met.
But he'd seen him in action, again and
again on tv.
And to him the demise of the hero
Supermyth was a complete mystery.
The hero that ended the horrifying
Universe War Five.
A superhero that kept the human race
alive.
And now the boy superhero of this
new era.
Is about to face, his own real life
terror.

The Boy Superhero

When the Boy Superhero took to the sky.
A misnomer of sorts he wanted to defy.
He didn't like the saying that a superhero
had gone down.
But he needed evidence factual and sound.
So he didn't tell the others of his black box
video find.
He needed to do more research, so he
needed a lot more time.
So he kept the small black box on his
person.
That would lessen the chance of anything
going wrong.
He didn't want it to be considered mistrust.
And he didn't know the Martians had begun
attack plan M.A.R.C.U.S.
But he'd bring up the Supermyth for the
skies were looking weird.
And the Martian war declaration, he kind
of feared.

The Boy Superhero

Powerplex computers proclaimed the
Earth in grave danger.
Extreme atmospheric conditions
became stranger and stranger.
Extreme heat at first, then extreme
cold.
Boy Superhero acknowledges it as a
hindsight foretold.
It's the creature Agod he said, the
creature's causing all of this.
The same creature that caused the
downfall of the Supermyth.
Let's research the Supermyth's end
and then you'll see.
The final answers and solutions to
all this mystery.
It's the atmosphere said the heroes,
stop all your wishing.
Then they sent the Boy Superhero on
a climatology mission.

The Boy Superhero

Across vast lands, across every ocean.
Boy Superhero searched to pinpoint the
commotion.
Typhoons and twisters engulfed the
planet.
Causing human peasantry to just lie
down and quit.
Whirlwinds galore, hail storms and
darkened skies.
Was this a meditated evil, with some
element of suprise.
Flyovers above Earth's atmosphere to
somehow overcome.
Disaster looming over the world, from
where did it come from.
His duty acknowledged, while the other
heroes defend.
The people and population from
possible dangers within.

The Boy Superhero

Unable to subdue the storm, he
rembered what next to do.
So he swam all the raging oceans and
all of deep sea blue.
Went below the ocean depths, to where
no human eyes would ever see.
To discover the secrets and teachings
of climatology.
After finding an ancient cavern, and
an antique old book.
Heard a knock in the darkness,
proceeded to take a look.
Seeing no one or anything, he began
to read the book.
Again he heard a noise, and again he
took a look.
Then instantly appeared Time Beings, one
then another.
Boy Superhero trounced one, then on to
thrash the others.

His premonition had been right and he
thought told you so.
Wanted to return to tell the heroes,
but before he could go.
He noticed a distress from Quasar 9.
Ventured toward that planet to see
what conflict he would find.
Not curious enough to track the Time
Beings and the battle interest gone.
Sped towards Quasar 9 to see what
was going on.
Time Beings evolved from Agod, the
creature joined at the side and the back.
Now the heroes of the era must
requisite their facts.
The Boy Superhero's brawl had been
quite a suprise.
One that will definetly be a clash to
analyze.

His distress bleeps and blinks alerted
the other heroes too.
Swytestar from Earth and Goodness
from Aquaplue.
Boy Superhero knew that he'd
arrive first.
The commotion of course would be
at its worse.
He'd seen practical jokes, pranks and
tricks.
But this had serious implications, this
was Universe War Six.
The Time Beings were after something and
they're connected to Agod.
He knew from his Supermyth research, that
he may have many issues to resolve.

Universe War Five
Universe War Six

Swytestar noticing two others answering
the distress.
Delayed leaving to concentrate on the
climatic mess.
Powergent decided to go examine the
infamous space shuttle.
Listening to battle tapes of the
Supermyth of low grumbles and mutter.
After observing the shuttle and bringing
the recordings to analyze.
Heroes of the era had a shocking
surprise.
Constant Anselm himself had walked
through the Powerplex.
Constant said Camille, young man give
us the facts.
You answered the distress to Quasar 9.
Swytestar delayed to see what you and
Goodness would find.

Well said Swytestar, I'd better go.
Goodness would be pretty upset, if
she's the only one to show.
Constant smiled, Camille said this is
not amusing.
In fact said Camille, it's quite confusing.
While Powergent reviewed the tapes of
the Supermyth.
Constant walked over and said here use
this.
What is it said Camille, what is that
thing on your arm.
It almost looks as though it could do
you harm.
He pushed a button , the Powerplex
began to glow.
Powergent got up, said, I've got to go.

What's going on said Camille, where did
he go.
Pyrotechnics said Constant, let's watch
the show.
Powergent she began to say, I didn't
realize...
Powergent starcar took to the skies.
Once the starcar was into full flight.
The Powergent starcar exploded out of
sight.
Now said Camille, you'd tell me where
you've been.
This little charade has got to end.
This is no game , the Powergent is
gone.
And don't ask me again, what's going
on.

Constant said Camille, what are you
saying.
Answer me please, stop all of your
playing.
Stop calling me that he said, it's
just the two of us.
From now on, you'll be calling me simply
Marcus.
Marcus she said, Constant, now listen.
Let me use a little super heroine intuition.
You've figured the secrets of climatology.
That still doesn't explain Swytestar and
Powergent to me.
Yes he said, exactly my dear friend.
Maybe I'm an alien or maybe Martian.
Camille was sickened, acknowledging
that an invasion had begun.
And she knew Universe War Six was
soon to be going on.

Universe War Six

On my arm said the android is my arsenal.
Each button is for a specific call.
Agod, Safirelapid, Time Beings, or
Martians.
Pick any button , where shall I begin.
You said Safirelapid she said, but he's on
confined on Quasar 9.
Explain that to me, I have plenty of
time.
What said Marcus, have you been asleep.
The first distress call, blink,blink bleep.
Yes said Camille, then three heroes are
headed there.
I'm sure no one there has anything to
fear.
The distress said Marcus our creature
has already attacked.
Crushing Quasar 9 and freed
Safirelapid as a matter of fact.

Snakeman then located where the Earth's
center is crystalized.
3000 miles into the Earth to unleash the
power of his laser eyes.
So when you hit a button, the Powerplex
became a deadly place to be.
You got that right lady, see the
Powergent flee.
Then Martian ships were waiting when the
starcar hit the sky.
Farewell to the hero, kiss the Powergent
bye-bye.
Well, I'd better get the Swytestar to
return now.
If anyone can end this, he'll know how.
Don't even try lady, don't even try.
Remember Safirelapid, these buttons,
Agod's in the sky.

Swytestar will have to help the other
two with our monster.
And guess what will be going on while
he's not here.
Time Beings and aliens, Martian ships will
flood the skies of the Earth.
Soon human existence will have no
value or worth.
She knocked the creature out, crushed
his arm and said all through.
Then contacted the Lifestar of Aquaplue.
As she thought of the dangers of which
the Lifestar would embark.
The Powerplex itself, became pitch
black and dark.
Wow she said, I've been here before.
Then she turned on intruder alert and
waited for what was in store.
Lower chamber abode had power recreated.

Stargistacola all alone, simply waited.
The Marcus creature awakened, said
lady what did you do.
She said contacted the Lifestar of
Aquaplue.
Said Marcus, there are many Martian
ships not that far away.
Flee now lady, I won't force you to stay.
Once they're here, they'll find their way in.
No way you and the Lifestar could possibly
win.
She said intruder alert is pretty efficient.
And help for the Lifestar has been sent.
No one's leaving or coming in and I can
take care of you.
When the Lifestar get's here, we'll decide
what to do.
Lifestar was about to land his
starcar on the moon.
Seeing the Earth invaded by Martian ships,
he had to plan real soon.

Universe War
Five

Quasar Nine

The Boy Superhero arrived on Quasar 9.
Utter destruction is what he did find.
Blackmania greeted him with a sense of
relief.
Our planet he said has suffered
enormous grief.
Safirelapid the snakeman must have
been in cahoots.
That creature that freed him is still
on the loose.
Before you arrived boy hero, all
hope seemed dim.
Direct me said the boy hero, I'll
take care of him.
The boy hero saw the creature, said
the Zymen have a look of fear.
He walked a step closer, said get the
Zymen out of here.

Zymen said Blackmania, your efforts
can now cease.
The Boy Superhero will battle the
beast.
The boy hero flew up , the creature
took a swing.
Boy Superhero proceeded to taunt the
thing.
He flew at the beast, then up, down
and around.
Then head on at the beast, the big
creature went down.
The Boy Superhero went over to
shake Blackmania's hand.
The creature barely moved, then it
began to stand.

Whoa! Said the boy hero, with arms
folded and humming.
I honestly have to say, I didn't see this
coming.
The boy hero flew up, the creature met
him in mid air.
Boy hero pounded the beast with more
than the beast could bear.
The creature fell, it had met it's fate.
Zymen and Blackmania began to
celebrate.
Boy Superhero was adorned, but again
once more.
The creature got up to an enormous roar.
The boy hero paced around, said I can
fight no longer.
The more it fights, it becomes even
stronger.

Quasar Nine

Zymen said Blackmania, contain the
beast, go to any length.
No said the Boy Superhero, I must
stop it from accruing strength.
Very well said Blackmania, tell us what
do you surmise.
I will defeat it said the boy hero, then
take it away before it begins to rise.
With his plan in motion , unchanged
and intact.
Boy hero would remove the beast from
the planet and alone he'd come back.
Very well said Blackmania, we'll see
you very soon.
I'll drop the beast in a black hole or some
distant moon.
Then we'll wait here for the Swytestar,
then on to track the snakeman.
Genius said Blackmania, one heck of a
plan.

Quasar Nine

Boy hero confronted the beast, hoping for
the last time.
But the beast hit the boy hero right on
the dime.
The boy hero didn't want a brawl or a
long bout.
He had to hurry up, for time was
running out.
He hit the beast squarely, the beast fell
on it's face.
Then he grabbed it and rushed it into
deep space.
Once deep into space, the creature
began to stir.
Martian ships were everywhere.
A voice from ships saying release the
invincible Martian.
Your days as a hero are about to end!

Universe War Five

Heroine Goodness

Goodness the heroine arrived on Quasar
Nine.
The Boy Superhero, she did not see or
find.
She conferred with Blackmania, and he
filled her in.
He told her how the creature got up
time and time again.
How the boy hero would drop it in deep
space and come back.
Assuring that the creature would never
ever again attack.
Then high above the Quasar 9 skies.
A figure appeared, quite a surprise.
Goodness looked up, said me, oh dear
my.
That is not the Boy Superhero in your
Quasar 9 sky.

Heroine Goodness

Goodness did research, so as to do no
wrong.
She did not want the beast to continue
to grow strong.
But she had to hurry, the beast was
probably not going to leave.
So she had to have something up her
sleeve.
Marce Invincible is what the creature
was called.
Built by Agod and Martians to never
permanently fall.
Virtually invincible and enormous in
size.
And adequately packaged with laser eyes.
That was the clincher that sealed her fate.
She told Blackmania, they should
patiently wait.

Heroine Goodness

The beast went into a rampage on Quasar
Nine.
Anything in it's path, simply went flying.
The creature crushed buildings and
defeated Zymen with ease.
Blackmania distraught, did not seemed
please.
Then he said, I myself will attack.
Goodness stopped him and held him
back.
Swytestar will be here, she said really
I'm sure.
We must not strengthen that creature
anymore.
But the creature led a relentless attack.
Finally Goodness decided that she must
now act.

She asked for help from Zymen volunteer.
Willing to fight with her without any fear.
The main objective was to help shield
the creature's laser eyes.
Three Zymen volunteered to her surprise.
The three Zymen kept the creature's
attention.
While Goodness pounded it into
submission.
The creature went down, but they knew
what was next.
The creature bounced up like a muscle
reflex.
But they had to hold on until Swytestar
arrived.
Simply contain the beast and stay alive.

The savage beast got up, went into a tear.
Zymen went at it without any fear.
One Zymen was crushed in the midst of
the beast's grip.
Two Zymen were left for the beast to
whip.
The two Zymen carried the beast into
space.
One disintergrated after being hit,
vanished without a trace.
The third Zymen fought on until
Goodness joined in.
Then Goodness downed the beast with
help from the last Zymen.
The heroine watched the beast so as not
to be caught by surprise.
The beast downed the heroine with his
laser eyes.

Universe War Five

Lifestar

Lifestar on the moon could see the
Earth real clear.
Starcar computers showed him what
was going on there.
He saw Martian ships everywhere.
He sensed the anxiety and agitation of
human fear.
He knew Stargistacola had her hands
full.
And that the necessity of the distress
call was no bull.
But he had to join her to plan any kind
of attack.
He had to get by the Martians and to the
Powerplex.
He calculated and navigated, then the
starcar was aloft.
A few quick adjustments, and the
starcar was off.

He converted Transformer starcar to a
streak of light.
A rapid flash zoom and the starcar was
out of sight.
Instantly without notice, the Lifestar
had arrived.
What was he about to face, once inside.
Intruder alert honed the Lifestar.
Stargistacola saw him, but didn't
interfer.
Help him said Marcus, let him in.
Or let your very own Powerplex destroy
your very own friend.
Stargistacola did not want to turn off
automatic intruder alert.
And she did not want to see the Lifestar
get hurt.
Here said Lifestar in Powerplex Flightport.
Just a second, I'm doing a little planning
of sorts.

Starcar said Lifestar, what is the danger.
Intruder alert said starcar, out here you're
a stranger.
Marcus looked on, then began to laugh.
Said come on Lifestar, tear the walls in
half.
Not a bad idea, Lifestar said.
Computer of the starcar , penetrate
the walls instead.
Stargistacola saw starcar computers take
the Lifestar's picture.
Rearranged his molecules and put him
right beside her.
Wow good trick, good trick said the
alien.
Do it in reverse, go back again.
No time said Lifestar, Stargistacola what
are you with!
He calls himself Marcus, the root cause
of all this.

Lifestar

111

He says he's Marcus, and that thing on
his arm.
Has already accounted for much havoc
and harm.
It's connected to Safirelapid, Agod and
the Martians.
And some other kind of beast, is where
the plot deepens.
A creature the boy hero went to Quasar
9 to meet.
Called Marce Invincible which Marcus
claims the boy hero can't defeat.
Then we won't expect help from Swytestar,
the boy hero or any cavalry.
We figure it out together, just you and
me.
I see that the alien's arm has been some
what disabled.
We plan around that in conjuction with a
 past hero's fable.

It's been said that the Supermyth was
very much alive.
The hero and the victor of Universe War
Five.
He destroyed Martian ships almost
effortlessly.
Kept human existence safe and free.
It's been said that Agod caught him by
surprise.
Without the chemical agent, the Supermyth
may have won and survived.
So said Marcus, one of you take Agod,
the other take the Martians.
That still leaves the Quasar 9 beast
and Safirelapid my friends.
We're not your friends said Lifestar,
we'll figure this out yet.
We still have the heroes Swytestar and
Llygentsheintshet.

Universe War Five

Aquaplue Foursome

The boy hero was surrounded, while the
monster returned to Quasar 9.
Boy Superhero was running out of
time.
Martian ships became stationary,
then unleashed a relentless attack.
Boy hero thrusted, fell abruptly back.
Weakened and stunned, but before it
had gone too far.
The Boy Superhero became a
Powerstar.
He quickly approached the ships,
toppled one then another.
Then dominoed effect of one into
the other.
Space junk he declared for all it
was worth.
Then smashed the ships once more
and headed to Earth.

Aquaplue Foursome

The boy hero saw the Earth, it seemed
worse than he had ever seen.
Stargistacola saw him approaching on
the Powerplex monitor screen.
The boy hero hesitated, he saw Agod.
The two halves separated, then a
confirming nod.
Each half roamed one half of the Earth
skies.
Martian ships suddenly began to rise.
Lifestar began out, Stargistacola
yelled no.
Marcus began to laugh, said help
him hero, go.
Hundreds of Martian ships blasted
boy hero's chest.
Boy Superhero was being put to
the test.

Lifestar started out again, but before he
could go.
Agod in tandem with Martians levelled
and dropped the Boy Superhero.
The boy hero fell to the ocean depths.
Marcus uttered quietly, two heroes
left.
Lifestar was about to take to the skies.
The Martian android activated his
laser eyes.
The Lifestar grew weak, the Martian
lasered him again.
Stargistacola glass encased the alien.
I'm going out there said Stargistacola,
I fear that the boy hero is dead.
Wait said the Lifestar, don't do
anything you'll later dread.

Stay here, stay calm, don't do anything
you'll regret.
He's still the Boy Superhero
Llygentsheintshet.
Wow said Stargistacola, this is a
nightmare.
Lifestar you're weak, I don't see
Llygentsheintshet anywhere.
Just then then boy hero returned to
the skies.
A look of shear anger in his eyes.
He crushed a dozen ships, then
hundreds more came.
Lifestar lay weak said, I am to
blame.
He stumbled helplessly into and
amongst the other rooms.
For the Boy Superhero, disaster looms.

Lifestar said Stargistacola, but he was
not replying.
Give up lady said Marcus, stop all
your trying.
The boy hero had recovered and
Agod was thoroughly pounded.
Once again Martian ships had the
boy hero surrounded.
Stargistacola could only watch
from the Powerplex monitor.
All action ceased, her heart was
tore.
Would her going out there help slow
the invasion.
Or where the heroes faced with an
impossible situation.
She watched her boy hero glide
in the air and ponder.
From the Powerplex monitors,
she dared to wander.

The ships all commenced fire, a direct
bullseye.
Stargistacola watched, almost a tear in
her eye.
The boy hero Powerstarred, and spread
his arms.
But the relentless attack was still doing
harm.
Then everything went black, the
Powerplex too.
Boy hero dropped to the ocean, then off he
flew.
After the pitch blackness came an
awesome blinding light.
Boy hero flying off, quickened the
pace of his flight.
After the blinding light came
hurricane force winds and a cloud mist.
What's going on yelped Stargistacola,
what is all this.

The Powerplex power was the only
power to come back.
The rest of the planet remained pitch
black.
Stargistacola came a voice, we are
here to help you.
We have tracked the Lifestar of
Aquaplue.
She saw four beautiful females
standing on the moon.
Promising to restore the Earth and
prevent it's doom.
Marcus looked on, yelling the Earth
will fall.
How can those four help with
anything at all.
A skeptic said the females, why is
he there.
Alien said Stargistacola, tries to control
his war from here.

Then said the heroines, we'll come
there with you.
We'll analyze the thing, to see what
we can do.
Marcus smirked as Stargistacola went
through details of the snakeman.
Very well said the heroines, we'll do
from here what we can.
We are Darkness, Swiftness,Lightness,
and Fondness, so true.
We will save the Earth with the help
of you.
Stargistacola smiled, it seemed
like a miracle.
The four heroines on the moon
formed a circle.
One within the circle would go to
kneel.
The other three around her formed a force
field.

The one within the circle extended her
arm straight and narrow.
Then her hand pointed to the sky like an
arrow.
Wow said Stargistacola, we might win
without fighting.
Then the heroine in the middle began
reciting.
People of the Earth, listen and hear.
Your planet has been divided into
four hemispheres.
People of my hemisphere of my
quadrant divide.
You will defeat the aliens with me on
your side.
I am Darkness and by my darkness
you are greeted.
Remain safe within darkness until
all aliens are defeated.

Aquaplue Foursome

I am Darkness and my actions will be
repeated.
By my fellow comrades until Earth's
problems are depleted.
Martian ships launched fire that was
lost in the dark of the night.
The ships and Agod could not attack
without light.
People of the hemisphere began to
move around.
Quiet and peaceful, without making a
sound.
She got up and Swiftness went to a
kneel.
People of the Earth, feel what I
feel.
The energy and swiftness of my
winds.
Agod nor the aliens will affect you
again.

Aquaplue Foursome

Martian ships collided in the winds.
People of the hemisphere had energy
again.
Agod's attack went wild and astray.
People of the Earth were finding their
way.
Swiftness stopped, Lightness began.
Lightness shows the way Earth human.
People of my hemisphere of my
quadrant.
Do anything you please, and don't
think you can't.
Follow the light of my lightness without
dismay.
We together in unison will send the
aliens away.
Martian ships were simply lost in the light.
Agod's attack plan evaporated from
sight.

Aquaplue Foursome

Once Lightness was done, Fondness
acted on cue.
The beautiful heroines were almost
through.
People of the Earth, I do love you so
dear.
Ignore the aliens and Agod without a
care.
I need from my hemisphere much
undivided attention.
And I grant you my fondess, and
the power of love intervention.
In my comrades and I, will you place
your trust.
Place the palm of your hand on your
computer screen thus.
Recite my love for Fondness is her love
for me.
Obtain this love and be alien free.

Aquaplue Foursome

Humans began to hug and love, shun Agod
and the aliens.
Fondness had created a hemisphere of
total friends.
Then she said each hemisphere has it's own
 protection.
Me and my comrades will now proceed
with unification.
So the heroines now promise to bring back
Earth's normalcy.
Get rid of the aliens and keep the
Earth free.
Stargistacola adjusted monitors to
attain the best view she could get.
Stargistacola said Marcus, care to make
a bet.

Universe War Five

Swytestar

Swytestar

Goodness was weak, but alive at least.
Blackmania tried to subdue the beast.
The beast had gotten more stronger
than ever.
And Blackmania didn't want the beast to
attempt to crush her.
The beast grabbed Blackmania and he
was thrown thump to the ground.
Blackmania lay there without
making a sound.
Goodness went to him, he whispered, it's
good Leda has fled.
Said 'The two moons' and closed, his
eyes, Blackmania was dead?
Goodness flew at the beast with all her
remaining strength.
She had to stop it, go to any length.
Severly weak, but she had to try.
The beast swatted Goodness like
a little fly.

Swytestar

Goodness fell from the sky, felt the
demoralizing end.
Then came a touch, got you my friend.
It was Swytestar the Superhero, and
Goodness was at ease.
Stop the beast said Goodness, please
Swytestar please.
Swytestar looked up, the pleasure
is all mine.
Earth is in peril, we don't have much
time.
Swytestar downed the beast, said
where's the fun what's the trick.
Stick around said Goodness, it's
no picnic.
Yeah came a voice and it'll get
stronger yet.
Approaching them from the air was
Llygentsheintshet.

I'm back said the boy hero, I 'm finally
back.
You know I couldn't even get to the
Powerplex.
The Earth is almost conquered that I do
fear.
Martian and alien ships are everywhere.
I was battling the Martians, almost
overcome in fact.
Then all of a sudden, the entire planet went
black.
Aquaplue Foursome said Goodness, they're
there to assist.
They can handle the Earth, while we take
care of this.
Boy hero said Swytestar, changed your
mind again.
While we hang in the balance, you research
the Supermyth's end.

Swytestar confronted the boy hero,
calling him a mere Earthling.
I've been here said the boy hero, battling
this beast of a thing.
A little thanks, congratulations at least.
I mean like she said that is surely no
picnic of a beast.
I don't get it said Swytestar, confused at
best.
Boy Superhero, quickly tell me the rest.
What is it said Goodness, what don't
you get.
Why are you questioning
Llygentsheintshet!
He was at the Powerplex, said he had
changed his mind.
It delayed my coming here to Quasar 9.

Swytestar

Swytestar secretly asked Goodness to
provoke a fight.
To hit the boy hero, with all her might.
Goodness obliged and the boy hero went
down.
Boy Superhero got up and looked around.
Before they knew it the boy hero was in
flight.
He came down on the heroine and called
the act trite.
Boy hero then said, you've got me wrong.
I've been here battling the beast all along.
Swytestar walked away, the boy hero
looked on.
Goodness said Swytestar, we have to know
what is wrong.
Swytestar walked away again, then began
to shout.
Why in the world, can't I figure this out!

Swytestar

Wait said Goodness, I've been meaning to
tell you.
We got a severe distress call on Aquaplue.
It said, Boy Superhero, just my luck.
I think my starcar is about to destruct.
Sparky said Swytestar, Perseus, the
Powergent.
The boy hero jumped in, I'll tell you
 where I went.
Swytestar walked away, said tell us where
you've been.
Goodness consoled, then embraced him.
Quickly boy hero, tell us then.
Goodness jumped in, we were all
Powergent's friend.
It's the end Swytestar, this day finally came.
We the heroes of this era are all to blame.
They all sat down, a day of lost glory.
Boy Superhero began to tell his story.

Swytestar

He told of the video black box, and the
Time Beings attack.
He told of the Martians, two moons, and
detailed every little fact.
He told of the shuttle, Marcel and Marce.
He said the anger of the Martians was
probably no farce.
When he concluded, he asked if the
Swytestar was mad.
Swytestar said no, and rub the boy hero's
head.
He said he'd gathered enough information
to possibly destroy the monster.
To efficiently get it done, and get out of
there.
The 3 heroes agreed, and all then smiled.
Let's do it said Swytestar, Earth's been
waiting for a while.

Swytestar

Swytestar went at the beast and
pounded it good.
Then he downed the beast and over
it he stood.
The beast got up in a furious rage.
Boy hero said Swytestar this beast
needs to be caged.
I tried once said the boy hero to take it
into deep space.
But Martian ships are everywhere out
to conquer the human race.
The Martians said Swytestar, we have
to get back to Earth.
This beast of a monster is more trouble
than it's worth.
The beast lasered the Swytestar, the
hero fell.
Llygentsheintshet attacked it to give
Swytestar a spell.

We're in trouble said Goodness, no way
to beat it.
Marce Invincible, no way to defeat it.
Just then the monster opened his fists.
Grabbed the boy hero and clutched him
in his midst.
Swytestar looked up, said hang in their
son.
Swytestar Powerstarred and the true
battle had begun.
He flew at the beast, then ripped off an
an arm.
Assuring that the monster could do the
boy hero no harm.
Then he ripped off the other arm and
Goodness began to laugh.
Then the three of them together broke
the monster in half.

Top half of the beast still had laser
eyes.
It locked on to Swytestar, knocking him
from the skies.
Get in the starcar , he told Goodness,
go hurry go.
Go help the Earth, we will soon follow.
The boy hero grabbed the top half, but the
laser traction didn't break.
Swytestar had only one path to take.
Powerstar mode against laser eyes.
As Swytestar grew closer the boy hero
saw their demise.
The laser eyes grew more potent as the
Swytestar closed in.
Then the spectacle and sound of an
enormous explosion.

Thundering sounds and a flash of bright.
Prompted Goodness in the starcar to
speed out of sight.
What was she doing what had she done.
Where they telling her to go help or
flee and run.
She wasn't sure but felt plenty of
  remorse.
And in her starcar, she plotted the
Earth course.
What really happened on Quasar 9.
Through space and on Earth, what
would she find.
She searched starcar computers for
her answers.
To have a means of defense as she
travelled there.

Universe War Five

Conclusion

Conclusion

Stargistacola watched the heroines as
they controlled the aliens at will.
Agod and the Martian ships remained
perfectly still.
Agod tried to figure the heroines antics and
force field.
Earth's fortune and good fate was
about to be sealed.
Fondness knelt down, the other three
around her.
People of the Earth, we're removing
all your fear.
We're removing your dread and
ending your fright.
And replacing it with the calm that
comes with the darkness of night.
Agod commanded Martian ships but
to no avail.
Again Martian ships would only fail.

Conclusion

We've brought you Lightness to lighten
your way.
To end Martian intrusion and end your
dismay.
This time when the Martians could
not handle the command.
Agod sent out a plea to the snakeman.
Safirelapid he said, from 3000 feet
below.
Make the Earth planet an entire
inferno.
Stargistacola was in awe, all people
became crazed.
Safirelapid the snakeman had set
the planet ablaze.
Agod took charge , Martians took
captives.
Fondness had given it all she
could give.

Stargistacola finally took flight, the war
was on.
Stargistacola said Marcus, good-bye,
so long.
The heroines to their assigned
hemisphere.
To help their Earth friends battle
from there.
Darkness brought gloom, then
cleared it away.
Then had her hemisphere hidden
away.
Lightness brought the path to light
the way.
And kept them within light without
disheartening or dismay.

Conclusion

Swiftness brought the breeze of
a cool day.
Swift winds to blow their troubles
away.
She kept them behind her high force
winds.
Then soothed their nerves over and over
again.
But Fondness and her cherished love
had been foiled.
The love of the Earth people, she
could not recoil.
Then in astonishment, she said help
me somehow.
Perseus, my comrade please right now.
But Perseus was gone, but she
continued with head in bow.
Come to me please, someway,
somehow.

She closed her eyes for a brief
moment.
And fell to the ground, no Powergent.
Goodness in her starcar finally arrived.
Hoping her friend Fondness was still alive.
She saw Agod in the pitch black night.
In her starcar they hid out of sight.
Agod was there, but made a quick shift.
It's movement was sudden, fast and swift.
Agod darted left and half darted
right.
Then an incredible detonation in the
middle of the night.
Goodness saw Martian ships, more coming
to attack.
Stargistacola crushed numerous ships, then
remembered the Powerplex .

Conclusion

When she returned to the Powerplex,
it was in shambles.
The price to pay, when you have to
gamble.
Intruder alert had been disengaged.
And the aliens had turned loose savagery
and rage.
In the blinking lights and quiet dark
of the Powerplex.
Stargistacola mulled about wondering
what was next.
A figure dropped from the ceiling
above.
She pondered what this may have
been in lieu of.
Marcus she exclaimed, is that you.
It's over heroine came a voice, there's
nothing you can do!

Then a figure pulverized her
as she crashed to a wall.
Cautiously she got up from her erratic
fall.
Deja vu she thought, as she had got up
from her fall and roll.
Powerplex computers flashed Agod is in
control.
Agod was in the Powerplex without
Swytestar and Powergent.
Is the Omnipotence Era done, never
again to be resurgent.
Agod made his way to Stargistacola,
the boy figured followed.
A hesitation in the heroine's motion,
she lightly swallowed.
It's over said Agod, read the computer
and weep.
The Earth and it's people are mine
to keep!

Conclusion

It's a nightmare said Stargistacola,
a teribbly bad dream.
Things cannot be happening the way
this all seems.
Agod closed in on Stargisacola with
the boy along side.
Both keeping in pace matching stride
for stride.
The boy put his hand on Stargistacola's
forehead.
I know this is distasteful, and a point
in time you've dread.
But its give up time , so lets not
try to fabricate.
Let's get on with the solutions, no
need to procastinate.
Then he slapped her shoulder stepped
away.
Time to end old frustrations what can we
say.

Give me your arm saidAgod, I need to
instruct the others as what to do.
It's over said the boy, especially for you.
Agod was annihilated by the boy heros
fist.
Then he took it's head a gave it a twist.
Threw the half of the creature aside
like a rag doll toy.
Then looked at Stargistacola smile with
joy.
Constant, she explained, where have
you been.
Just out on a little climatolgy mission.
Quiet he said, it's not over yet.
Boy hero came a voice,
Llygentsheintshet.
That's me said the boy hero, what's it
to you.
I see the end said the voice, the end
so true.

Conclusion

Just one of you said the boy hero and
two superheroes.
But look at the computer monitor, he
said, still many of foes.
Check the other room and who do you
see.
Powergent said the boy hero, but how
can that be.
What is it said Stargistacola rubbing
her face and head.
Powergent is back there, but I
can't tell if he's alive or dead.
We can handle you, said the
boy hero and plus there's two of us.
We'll finish you off and the Martians,
if we must.
Stargistacola looked at the monitor,
the planet ablazed.
Enough talk said Stargistacola, here
out of our way.

Not so fast said another voice, a female companion.

Two to Two said the boy hero, but we heroes will still win.

Zymedes said the female, tell me , how are you alive.

Well this is the time you finally die.

Zymedes said the boy hero, what's going on.

Then the female raised her hand and extended her arm.

The figure she had called Zymedes, she had begun to laser.

Agod became conscious and began to commend her.

Zymedes crouched began to stumble and fall.

Swytestar the Superhero tore through the wall.

Swytestar blocked the laser and became a Powerstar.

It's the end said Agod, you know who we are.

Then the Marcus creature came around and began with the laser.

Stargistacola subdued Agod as Swytestar had hoped of her.

It's the end Swytestar, just say it's the end.

The two alien Martians lasered in tandem.

Conclusion

You're forgiven said the Swytestar, to the
Boy Superhero.
Wipe them out and said I told you so.
The boy hero crushed Marce and then said
oh heck.
Flew up and down and around the
Powerplex.
Then in the center of the Powerplex the
boy hero stood.
Finally he flashed towards the Marcus
android and put him out for good.
What was that Stargistacola said with a
grin.
I just wanted to get a good look at him.

Conclusion

Lifestar said the Swytestar, come on in here.

The Powerplex lit up, the Lifestar was there.

It wasn't enough to see Lifestar the hero.
Two beautiful ladies were soon to follow.
Goodness and Fondness casually walked in.

Said now my hero friends, where shall we begin.

Help the Powergent said Swytestar, he needs to be revived.

So he can ask the Boy Superhero about Universe War Five.

The boy hero laughed, said, but really are you alright.

Sure said Swytestar, want to try me in a fight.

Conclusion

No said the boy hero, you know fighting is
not my style.
I think I'll kick back and mess with
computers for a while.
The heroes all laughed again, happy as
could be.
The boy hero called to Swytestar in secrecy.
Then Swytestar yelled across the room,
Fondess, who is that with you.
Fondness yelled back, maybe a man from
Aquaplue.
Zymedes walked over to Constant,
whispered, who's she with.
Why I'm Effin Babbles Lecastle, the
Supermyth!
Zymedes walked towards the others and
they all walked away.
Boy Superhero just stood there, what did I
say!

Epilogue

Epilogue

Heroes of the era didn't like talking about
Universe War Five.
Whether or not the Supermyth hero was
dead or alive.
In fact their feelings were always a little
mixed.
Until they became involved in Universe
War six.
It happened so fast they were never really
sure.
Why it happened , what it was for
Throughout it all they learned to grieve.
And in each other, they learned to believe.
This is an era, humans will always choose.
An era of heroes, we shall never lose.
Heroes of an era, villains shall never defeat.
The Omnipotence Era and all of it feats.

Epilogue

Historians love to document wars.
However, there's no way to actually keep
score.
Sometimes there's fatalities, agony and
pain.
Sometimes if any, there's very little gain.
Because human existence is always
anxious to know.
And because there's heart in the real hero.
And because these heroes are difficult to
meet.
The heroes of the era have chronicled their
feats.
Because Universe War Six was no easy
effort.
Some heroes of the era, cut their stories
short.

Universe War Six Chronicled

Forthright Omnipotence Era

Five Point Powerplex

(Secret and Confidential)

Boy Superhero(Chronicled)
Constant Marcus Anselm:
Llygentsheintshet:

I am Constant Marcus Anselm, the Boy
Superhero, Llygentsheintshet.
Universe War Six are of battles we will
never forget.
I remember going on about UniverseWar
Five.
Whether or not the Supermyth hero was
still alive.

But the heroes were all busy with the crazy
atmosphere.
Weather so weird, they wouldn't lend me an
ear.
I remember trying to tie the two together.
You know, the death of Supermyth and the
mysterious weather.
Finally they got tired of listening to me.
And sent me on a mission of climatology.
I searched the skies, searched the rivers and
oceans.
Where man has been and never been.
I encountered Time Beings in a cavern
below ocean depths.
Received a distress call, so I demolished
the Time Beings and left.
The distress call came from Quasar 9.
It seemed important, so I didn't waste any
time.

I wasn't surprised to see that I was the first
one there.
Blackmania and the Zymen were full of
fear.
I got to the point where I could fight no
longer.
For whenever I downed the beast, it came
back stronger.
So I downed the beast and removed it from
Quasar 9.
Once in deep space, guess what I did find.
An entire slew of Martian ships.
But not too many for Boy Superhero to
whip.
The beast made its way back to Quasar 9.
But I was concerned with Earth and did not
have the time.

So when I finished off the Martian ships for
all it was worth.
I took my concerns and curiosity and
headed to Earth.
Earth looked frightening, captured in fact.
Did I have enough in me to launch an
attack.
Where were the heroes, Martian ships were
everywhere.
Only one way to find out, into the open
without fear.
Martian ships attacked, Agod had been
hiding.
Where they now ruling the Earth, or
wishfully presiding.
Then relentlessly they attacked, eminent
danger loom.
And just when I thought I was about to
face doom.

Earth went black, then intermittent
light flash.
I fell to the ocean in a whopping big splash.
Not caring to investigate and without fear
or fret.
I headed back to Quasar 9 to see if
Swytestar had arrived yet.
I saw Swytestar and Goodness, boy that
was relieving.
Now we got a team again, best believing!
Swytestar told Goodness, to go to Earth and
wait.
That we'd be there later to better their fate.
After that things began to happen so quick.
I'd rather not speak of it, it makes me sick.

Constant Marcus Anselm
The Boy Superhero
Llygentsheintshet
Universe War Six

Stargistacola(Chronicled)
Camille Leah Millicent:
Stargistacola: Super Heroine:

Constant kept bothering us about the
Supermyth.
I simply told him, we didn't have time for
all this.
So we let him do something to set his mind
free.
A complete global mission of climatology.

A distress call came from Quasar 9.
With the horrendous weather, we couldn't
find time.
But distress calls were always important we
know.
So we agreed that at least, one of us should
go.
Swytestar prepared to go, hopefully it
wouldn't take long.
We needed to figure out Earth's atmosphere
and what was going on.

Swytestar headed to the starcar and didn't
leave at all.
Said funny, seems like the Boy Superhero
has answered the distress call.
So we continued our strategy to combat
the global catastrophe.
Programming Powerplex computers to
figure out climatology.

Powergent stopped, said finally, at last.
I'm going to search the area of the
Supermyth crash.
He brought back a recording, a little black
box.
Said, bet you the information on this will
knock off your socks.
He reviewed the recording with Swytestar,
seemingly differing opinions.
Swytestar got up, say I just can't win.
Then the Boy Superhero walked in with a
 big smile.

Swytestar said, we thought you'd be gone
for a while.
Swytestar looked at him and said, this isn't
amusing.
When you answer a distress, don't make it
confusing.
Swytestar left, he seemed to hesitate.
Then he simply said, we'll discuss all this
at a later date.
I was confused, especially with that thing
on Constant's arm.
It seriously looked like, it could do some
serious harm.
He pushed a few buttons walking over
towards Powergent.
The Powerplex glowed somewhat and off
Powergent went.

The starcar had taken flight exceptionally
fast.
And right before my eyes, an outrageously
enormous blast.
Eventually he told me what I didn't want to
know.
He was a Martian boy impersonator with
Martian ships to follow.

So I crushed the device on his arm not
caring if it did or didn't hurt.
And set the entire Five Point Powerplex on
automatic intruder alert.

The sudden exits of Swytestar and
Powergent, not knowing either situation.
I confined myself to the Powerplex not
letting anyone or anything out or in.
Without a doubt, I needed help, this I must
confess.
Knowing the Earth was being invaded, I
sent out my own distress.
Powerplex monitors patrolled the Earth
giving a clear concise overall view.
Then I strategically planned and patiently
waited for the Lifestar of Aquaplue.
The Lifestar arrival was comforting, but
after that I can't say.
When I bring myself to grips with all this,
I'll finish it some day.

Camille Leah Millicent
Stargistacola
Universe War Six

Lifestar of Aquaplue(Chronicled)
Calmey Callimachus Vita:
Lifestar of Aquaplue: Mizar

I received three distress calls so I thought
the situation to be urgent.
Swytestar, Stargistacola and Powergent.
The Swytestar distress was of serious
concern.
Powergent's distress was of what he had
learned.
Stargistacola was frantic about what she
was with.
Swytestar's concern was of the Supermyth.
Calmey, Calmey Vita, he said.
This distress needs to be quickly read.

Calmey, Calmey Vita my friend.
Fellow hero and fellow Aquapluian.
Something is wrong at the Powerplex.
I haven't time to relay the facts.

Research the Supermyth of Universe War
Five.
Boy Superhero keeps asking, if he's still
alive.
I will leave my starcar at the moon.
You'll find an audio copied recording,
review it soon.
Stargistacola's message was a bit more
serious.
In the tune of hurry, hurry, hurry, you must!
Swytestar left to help Quasar 9.
And Powergent's starcar signal, I cannot
find.

He left in a hurry and I noticed an
explosion.
I dare not expand or further the notion.
An alien is here, he calls himself Marcus.
He says you won't help, but you'll be
plenty of help I trust.
Powergent's message was proof of real
trouble.
It came in an ejected missile time capsule.

The Powergent himself had been ejected
too.
But he was not headed for Earth or
Aquaplue.
After computing the facts, and doing my
math.
I knew there'd be hundreds if not thousands
of space crafts.

Before going to Earth I landed on the moon
surface.
The planet Earth looked like a defeated,
conquerable place.
Alien and Martian ships were everywhere .
I had to get to the Powerplex and take it
from there.
Starcar camouflaged itself as a streak of
light.
Instantly I was at the Powerplex and in
Stargistacola's sight.
I can't let you in she said, intruder alert is
set on automatic.
Do you have means of getting in here, some
type of tactic.

 I programmed starcar to recreate me as a
molecular shower.
Get me in the Powerplex for a little more
than an hour.

As a molecular shower starcar sent me in to
the Powerplex.
I had a little more than an hour before the
time molecules brought me back.
Once in the Powerplex, I solidified.
Stargistacola was overjoyed that I had made
it inside.
I used Powerplex computers to check the
circumstances.
Martian progress, movement, manuever and
advances.
As we planned our strategy against the
Martians, we suddenly realized.
The Martian Android was staring me down
with his eyes.
Then a laser flash, the Android's eyes let
loose a laser beam.
I was out for quite a while so it seems.

I remember staggering into the next room
and when I hadn't gone far.
Timed molecular brought me back to the
starcar.
I was weak and couldn't wait for starcar
recovery mode.
I had to go back into the Powerplex in the
lower chamber abode.
There I could recover at a much faster
speed.
To be able to do battle, full strength I would
need.
Once recovered starcar brought me back
for an update.
So much chaos and havoc, I'll continue at
a later date.

Lifestar of Aquaplue
Calmey Callimachus Vita
Mizar
Universe War Six

Goodness(Chronicled)
Goodness:
Heroine from Aquaplue:

I was headed for Quasar 9 on distress.
I became quite confused I must confess.
If Earth's heroes were to help Quasar 9.
A distress from them meant trouble big
time.
The message was sent from the Powegent.
Tagged and coded as extremely ugent.
Aquaplue filled me in before, they let
me go.
Was this the end of the Powegent hero.
Lifestar was enroute to investigate.
Would he get there before it was too late.
I continued on to Quasar 9.
What dangerous encounters would I find.

Blackmania greeted me on Quasar 9.
The Boy Superhero, I was hoping to find.
Blackmania assured me the boy hero would
be back.
The boy hero had warded off the beast's
relentless attack.
He told me Zymedes was the strongest of
the Zymen.
Though only half strength and never
wishing to fight again.
He told me Zymedes would always grow
weak.
Leda his friend would not let him speak.
She said she'd would always be his best
friend.
Stay by his side, to the end.
But she asked for Zymen escorts to take her
away.
She feared Quasar Nine would be gone
some day.

Zymedes fell sick, didn't want her to go.
So he said he'd volunteer to help any
incoming hero.

Before we knew it the monster was back.
Neither of us could slow the monster's
attack.
I was really glad, when Swytestar arrived.
A much better feeling of being alive.
The boy hero had a black box, that we
reviewed in detail.
Swytestar was sure that his plan would not
fail.

After reviewing the video the Swytestar
seemed pleased.
Me and the boy hero became much more
at ease.
He said that Llygentsheintshet had not
watched the entire video.
He was in too big a hurry to research the
Supermyth hero.
He said the two moons were not the two
moons of Mars.
Whether the two moons the Supermyth
used to research the stars.
Then he made mention of the shuttle
passengers.
Saying at least one of them may have been
right here.
He thought I should go to Earth to
investigate.
But first we'd bring down the monster
before it was too late.

Before we finished, he sent me to Earth to intervene.
The planet Earth was a horrible scene.
I saw Fondness barely moving and helped her revive.
I was glad my friend was still alive.
We eventually made our way to the Powerplex.
The entire planet was under attack.
The rest of the foursome was handling the fight.
While we ventured through the Powerplex in the pitch black dark of night.

Goodness:
Heroine from Aquaplue

Marcel(Chronicled)
Marcel:
Human:
Last Days on Earth:

Strange things are happening, so we have to write fast.

These writings of ours may be our last.

My wife and I declined the shuttle flight.

The mere mention of it sent her into fright.

During the war McCalsa took too long to intervene.

And the Supermyth hero was late on the war scene.

Though he was our friend we told him we couldn't go.

But when my wife turned on the tv, she screamed hell no!

She saw the two of us getting on board.

Please do help us, please help us lord.

He called the wife of McCalsa Televu.
She said, be attentive to anything and
everything around you.
There was a box outside on our porch.
And a light in the sky lit up like a torch.
We told her the box had a man's bracelet.
She said she was leaving, that was that.
We took the bracelet and threw it in the
yard of her home.
When we got back the sky lights hovered
and roamed.
We went inside and locked the door.
We're trembling from the knocking, we
can't write any more.

Marcel:
With his wife Marce:
Last days on Earth:

Powergent(Chronicled)
Spargont(Sparky) Brian Josephson:
The Powergent:
Perseus of Aquaplue:

I examined the shuttle, but it wasn't all there.
An audio black box without a video pair.
The shuttle itself was a burned out mess.
Surely there had been no survivors left.
But listening to the audio changed my mind.
Someone or something had been left behind.

At least three survivors seemed possible
after the explosion.
To any sane mind, it seemed like a far
fetched notion.
There was Marce, Marcel and Supermyth.
With video help I could have devised
something from this.

But my research had been interrupted by
the Boy Superhero.
What he had on his arm that day, I may
never know.
But when he approached and showed it to
me.
I never had a chance to clearly see.

Before I knew it, I had left my chair.
Headed towards my starcar to get out of
there.
I didn't have time to check on the others
well being.
But a whale of catastrophe, I'd began
seeing.
Hundreds of Martian ships flooded the
skies.
It was Universe War Six, I began to realize.
There was no such thing as good fortune or
luck.
I had to let the starcar deliberately destruct.
Before it did I sent a message to Aquaplue.
I may not be around, do all you can do.

Also I had sent a missle to the Ganymede
moon.
 I needed Aquaplue to do research on it
quickly and soon.
After that I ejected and the starcar was
gone.
Now the battle with the Martians was full
force and on.
After crushing many of their ships , I didnt
feel alright.
Martians had something efecting my
flight.
A flight diminisher ray, I could barely flee.
It was very effective, that much I could see.

Flight diminisher ray was powerful, the
Martians closed in.
I dropped from the sky and began my
hiding.
Flight was no longer possibe, but I lost
them during the chase.
Only Triad Powerstar could get me from
place to place.

So I Powerstar travelled to the old home
of Camille Millicent.
There I forgot all about being Powergent.
I could see Martian ships everywhere.
After resting a little, I used her computer.
Research gave me an idea of what to do.
So I Powerstarred to the old home of
McCalsa Televu.

I searched the yard and there I found it.
A box the aliens had left on the planet.
I took it back to examine the contents.
I needed to figure out what it meant.
I pulled it out, it was a man's bracelet.
That's as far as I would get.
Now I was crippled, I wouldn't go far.
I couldn't even travel by Powerstar.
My super powers greatly diminished.
As Powergent the hero, I may be finished.

The Powergent
Spargont(Sparky) Brian Josephson
Perseus
Universe War Six

Blackmania(Chronicled)
Blackmania:
Supreme Commander of Quasar 9

Zymen got news of a badly destroyed
shuttle.
Investigation required, reports of which
made it seem criminal.
Black box audio depicted merciless cries.
Zymen researching noticed a lurking figure
in the skies.
So as not to be followed or give away any
notion.
Zymen secretly removed the bodies and set
off another explosion.

Zymen paranoid of the lurking entity and
sensing fear.
Left the black boxes and removed two
passengers.
The male we called Zymedes, for he slept
talked Ganymedes moon all night.
The female we called Leda, a smaller moon
of the larger satellite.
Zymedes never hesitated to be by Leda's
side.
Whenever he asked for help Leda, would
abide.
Zymedes was always weak, something
neither of us could explain.
Leda would stay there with him to try to
ease his pain.

When the monster first attacked Zymedes
felt to blame.
Said if he'd ever gained some strength,
he'd fight it all the same.
Leda started to panic after the heroes began
to arrive.
She thought the heroes beaten and wanted
to leave alive.

So she asked me nicely one day, if I would
be so kind.
If she could have two Zymen escorts to
get her off of Quasar 9.
Of course I did oblige her and sent her on
 her way.
Reluctantly my Zymen, I have not seen to
this present day.

The heroine Goodness told me, Leda may
have been a farce.
She may have been the Martian android
of the description Marce.
I know the Swytestar is coming to help the
great heroine.
Regardless of my well being, I trust that
they will win.
I think I maybe dying, but in war that's how
it goes.
I place the fate of myself and my planet in
the hands these great heroes.

Blackmania
Supreme Commander of Quasar Nine
Universe War Six

Aquaplue Foursome(Chronicled)
Aquaplue Foursome:
Darkness: Swiftness
Lightness: Fondness
Heroines from Aquaplue:

We had received the Swytestar call and the Powergent too.
We had received Blackmania's initial call on Aquaplue.
The heroine Stargistacola had also sent an urgent call.
We put the puzzle of messages together and began to analyze them all.
When we arrived on Earth, the boy hero was being attacked.
Darkness used her powers to turn the entire planet dark and black.

We told Stargistacola, we would help the
heroes reign.
She told us she had a captive, that she was
keeping under watchful restrain.
We told her how our plan was to take shape
and unfold.
How Lifestar had computerized them to
every single Earth household.
Each of us, our special powers, would
preserve human life and intelligence.
From our computerized belts to household
computers our powers are dispensed.
We are Darkness, Lightness, Fondness,
and Swiftness, all from Aquaplue.
We are here for peace, here for life, here to
love all of you.
Although the initial plan faltered pretty
much near the end.
An all important message had reached
Fondness the heroine.

While in the act of securing, the safety of
her quadrant.
She received an important message on the
location of Powergent.
She told the heroine Goodness who told
the Supermyth too.
He'd get Powergent to the Powerplex and
we would all begin anew.
Goodness went with Fondness to a dark
Powerplex they found in ruin.
While hopefully we three outside can end
this war real soon.

Aquaplue Foursome
Darkness: Swiftness
Lightness: Fondness
Universe War Six

Swytestar(Chronicled)
Keith Karl Katz:
Swytestar the Superhero:
Sirius from Aquaplue:

The Boy Superhero was acting despicable.
He changed his mind about answering the
distress call.
So I made my way to Quasar Nine.
Not knowing what the Boy Superhero had
on his mind.

When I got there, there was a look of doom.
Everywhere I looked disaster loomed.
Goodness the heroine greeted me.
She said defeat of the monster was
becoming a hard thing to see.
I stepped around her and immediately
brought the beast down.
The monster out cold simply lay on the
ground.
As I returned to converse with her, we
received quite a surprise.
Boy Superhero came from the skies.
While the monster was out, we had time to
strategize.
After hearing about the Powergent, he got
a sad look in his eyes.
He then gave me a black box video.
Showing the shuttle demise of the
Supermyth hero.

I watched the video, it was helpful indeed.
I told the two of them, that it was what
we would need.
McCalsa was shown in deep meditation.
He must have thought Marce Attacker was
of his knowledge creation.
It showed how Supermyth crushed the
attacking android.
After that he became a hero to avoid.
The male android aboard the shuttle
jumped from the craft.
The female shut down it's functions on
the male's behalf.
The destroyed android was called Marce
Attacker.
Once Supermyth destroyed it, it could no
longer back her.
The android that had jumped was called
Marcel.
Agod attacked after that android fell.

200

After I watched the video I knew he hadnt
watched it entirely.
The boy hero only watched what he had
wanted to see.
He had given us a lot, we were able to plan.
We had to stop the beast from rising again.
Goodness left for Earth ahead of us.
The safety of the Earth, we placed in her
trust.
After that the monster was defeated.
Through a flash stream, by the
Supermyth I was greeted.
I told him to go ahead to give the Earth
another hero.
The boy hero and I would soon after follow
I told the boy hero to take the snakeman
out.
I myself, would knockAgod about.

One half of Agod slipped by me.
However the boy hero took out Safirelaid
brilliantly.
He would meet me at the Powerplex after
taking care of the Earth center.
I had told Supermyth to also have him and
Goodness meet there.
At the dark Powerplex, there was a lot of
bewilderment and confusion.
I'm not going into details, I'm just glad
we're all done.

The Swytestar
Keith Karl Katz
Sirius of Aquaplue
Universe War Six

Supermyth(Chronicled)
Effin Babbles Lecastle:
McCalsa Televu:
The Supermyth:
Zymedes:

I boarded the space shuttle after Universe
War Five.
Trying to keep the victory spirit alive.
I was hesitant to go, in fact I didn't want to.
My wife was persistent, saying don't do
what you don't want to do.
But as a hero I felt obligated and it was
only for one time.
My wife refused, and stayed behind.

All of our friends also refused.
Which is why once on the shuttle, I became
totally confused.
I did an alien scan of my very own friends.
Nothing there, so I settled on in.

Marce and Marcel were on the space ship.
Yes my two friends were making the trip.
Curiosity made me question them one time.
Yes they said McCalsa, we simply changed
our minds.
I asked Marcel about the two moons and
the stars.
He immediately began to speak of the
planet Mars.
Something outside the shuttle caused a loud
pop.
Marcel I said, but then I stopped.

204

Me, my wife and our friends in the past.
Would discuss the two moons while
having a blast.
We put in our discussions secretly.
What the mention of two moons would
ultimately be.
The Ganymede moon and the Earth moon
itself.
Without a doubt and nothing else.
The two moons most responsible for my
being who I was.
But now the words of Marcel have me
concerns of just cause.
Someone or something was absorbing the
knowledge of my mind.
But I saw nothing around of the android
kind.
Somewhere in my scanning, I must have
slipped.

So I put my mind solely on my dismantled
rocket ship.
When I looked outside the shuttle nothing
was there.
The entire group of passengers had a look
of constrained fear.
Another bump, then a devastating knock.
The entire space shuttle went completely
dark.
I took that moment to change to the
Supermyth hero.
Whatever was out there, just had to go.
A flying android, this could become a
nightmare.
I ripped at it without a care.
The android seemed to know my thought.
So I pulled it apart, before it fought.
I saw Marce and Marcel through the
shuttle window look on.

They didn't seemed pleased that the android
was gone.
In any case I headed back to go inside.
When a thunderous jolt hit my backside.
I turned to face it, and it blasted by chest.
This creature was about to experience my
best.
It split in half and went in separate
directions.
So I did the wise thing and went after one.
The one half I blasted, I mean I caught
good.
Turned around and looked and there the
other half stood.

Before I knew it, it had raised its hand.
It would be a while if before I become
full strength again.
The creature had blasted me into the shuttle
and by chance.

It had broken the encasement containing
the chemical substance.
Marce I said we've hit a space bump.
Marce wasn't joking, she said Marcel had
jumped.
That wasn't Marcel said Marce, instead he's
the cause of all this.
Now we all must die, including you
Supermyth.
She was right I felt weak, I knew we were
all done.
Nowhere for anyone to hide, flee or run.
Then the creature raised its hand again.
Another blast and that was the end.
 At some point in time I opened my eyes.
That in itself was an astounding surprise.

What had happened after the enormous
explosions.
On my mind where a couple of questions.
How the heck did I survive and was I out of
danger.

And the place itself couldn't look any
stranger.
Then I was approached by some human like
men.
They said my comrades were all dead,
except one remaining friend.
Zymedes they said, your friend Leda is
here.

She's been by your side providing you care.
Zymedes I said why are you calling me that.
Relax they said, try not to fret.
Throughout your sleep, you spoke of the
Ganymedes satellite.
All day long and into the night.
I told the rescuers I couldn't recall or
remember.
And as for the lady I didn't recognize her.
I don't know myself or her or any of you.
I have a lot to learn, really I do.

I am Blackmania, he said, and these are my
Zymen.
They've selected Zymedes for your name
and Leda for your friend.
Two moons from the solar system from
which you were found.

You'll be safe here feel free to move
around.
I saw a lot during my years on Quasar 9.
I saw the hero Swytestar visit one time.
He saved a heroine from certain death from
a deadly star.
I idolized that hero, but only from afar.
Then the beast came and the boy hero
arrived.
I promised I would help, if it meant keeping
him alive.
I like the boy superhero, he was a winner
through and through.
A champion of life reliable and true.

When he didn't come back and the beast
returned.
And the lovely heroine showed up with a
look of concern.

I started to remember who I was.
I had to lend a hand in the right of just
cause.
As I was helping I saw a streak of blue.
Before I knew it I had been brought to
Aquaplue.
8 heroines collapsed when I first reached
Aquaplue.
The heroine Brightness attributed it to
Vapor 5262.
They were monitoring the area and during
the fight.
They wanted to examine my body of light.
They told me I was sort of, of Aquapluian
descent.
I kind of sort of, knew what they meant.
They questioned me thoroughly and I
filled them in.
I told them I'd be going back to fight again.

They had me placed in a prismatic ellipse.
Until the effects of the Vapor 5262 had
been eclipsed.
I remember being flash streamed back to
Quasar 9.
That experience really blew my mind.
There were a bunch of bright lights and an
enormous explosion.
It seemed as if everything in the area was
totally gone.
When I cleared by eyes and looked around.
The Boy Superhero was out on the grouind.
Then from beyond the stars, I saw a figure
appear.
He came up to me and asked what are you
doing here.
I told him I was sent from Aquaplue.
And the boy hero was on the ground, was
there anything I could do.
I told them where I had been and how they
had informed me.

He said the planet Earth is where I needed to be.

He told me the heroine Goodness had been sent earlier.
Get there fast, there was urgency to find her.

He said he was Swytestar and he'd soon follow.
Once he looked after the Boy Superhero.
While flying to Earth. I had time to reminiscense.
What if the heroes prevail, and I become a part of all this.
Always working with Swytestar and the Boy Superhero.
A true authentic hero of the Omnipotence Era show.
Such an incredible an wonderful notion.
Just as incredible as the initial Super nova explosion.

And what of Leda, Marce all along.
Staying by my side while doing me wrong.
Zapping my strength, keeping me down.
Fleeing when the heroes came around.
Well forget the androids, I have my hero friends.
And it's off to find, Goodness the heroine.
When I found Goodness I found Fondness with her.
After that my head isn't really too clear.
I remember taking Powergent to the Five Point Powerplex.
After that I can't be certain of all the facts.

The Supermyth
Effin Babbles Lecastle
McCalsa Televu
Zymedes
Universe War Six

Afterword

At war's end Swiftness was asked to
provoke a conflict.
One that would bring out the hidden
Martian Mothership.
When Swiftness winds decreased and
her speed began to slow.
The Mothership was attacked by the
rest of the heroes.
Destroying it and the secrets to the
flight diminshing ray.
Assuring no hero would ever face it again
some day.
The prototype to the Martian Android
Control Unit Series.
Was also destroyed to relieve the Boy
Superhero of all his worries.

The genius of Supermyth to contemplate
disassemble on his mind.
Merely saved the existence of human kind.
If androids conquering the universe would
ever start.
Anyone strong enough was welcome to
rip them apart.
If it was to be his downfall, his end, his
demise.
There would still be a chance to deploy a
futuristic surprise.
Ordinary humans would have been simple
prey.
This is where the Omnipotence Era comes
into play.
This is the Supermyth, this was his story.
And how the heroes of the era, brought
him to full glory!

Glossary

Agod - Roams the skies looking for conflict. Back to back or side to side mystical creature. Super Villain.

Aquaplue Foursome - Four super heroines from Aquaplue with computerized belts and computerized black discs in the palm of their hands. Assembled for the sole purpose to end Universe War Six. Darkness, Fondness, Swiftness and Lightness.

Blackmania - Supreme commander of Quasar Nine.

Bluestream - Developed by Aquaplue to instantly retrieve a person or object from deep space.

Glossary

Earthling - Inhabitant of Earth.

Evanesce 36-8380 - A substance fatal to the heroes from Aquaplue

Five Point Powerplex - Location, headquarters of the heroes of the era.

Flashstream - The inverse of bluestream. Placing a person or object from Aquaplue to a specific place or destination.

Flightport - Starcar landing zone at the Powerplex.

Forthright Omnipotence Era - The new era of superheroes.

Glossary

Ganymede moon - Moon where Supermyth did research, and where his rocket ship crashed from a super nova collision.

Goodness - Heroine from Aquaplue. Heroines of the like of Brightness and the Aquaplue Foursome.

Lifestar - Mizar from Aquaplue. Calmey Callimachus Vita. Superhero

Llygentsheintshet - The Boy Super hero. Constant Marcus Anselm.

Marce - Martian Android Reality Control Expert. Female android that analyzes non android to calculate next maneuver. Newest breed of androids.

Glossary

Marce Attacker - Fying android of Marce used to attack space shuttle after Universe War Five. Lacked laser weaponry.

Marcel - Martian Android Robot Control Entity Link. Older breed of impersonating androids, used to link to the newer breed of reality control and laser weaponry.

Marce Invincible - Flying android of Marce used to attack Quasar 9. Equipped with laser eyes touted as unbeatable.

Marcus - Martian Android Reality Control Unit Series. Prototype slated for mass production. Equipped with laser arsenal and reality control shield.

Glossary

Powergent - Superhero. Perseus from Aquaplue. Spargont(Sparky) Brian Josephson.

Powerstar - Heroes of the era can attain additional strength and energy Simply love oneself, another hero or someone or something thus involved in heroism. Primarily the Triad Powerstar sourced by the Five Point Powerplex.

Quasar Nine - Home of Blackmania and his followers, the Zymen.

Stargistacola - Camille Leah Millicent. Super heroine.

Supermyth - McCalsa Televue, Victor of Universe War Five. Zymedes Effin Babbles Lecastle..

Glossary

Swytestar - Sirius from Aquaplue. Keith Karl Katz. Superhero.

Time Being - Humans captured by Agod and through mythical snakes and a type of metamorphose, retained life and obtained super strength. Super villain. (Snakes of Safirelapid).

Timed Molecular - Used by Lifestar to penetrate walls of the Powerplex.

UFO - Unidentified flying object. flying saucer.

Vapor 5262 - Chemical substance proven fatal to the Supermyth.

Zymen - Enforces of law and order on Quasar Nine.

Poetry

Haiku - Summertime

Violet concord...
White blue yellow purple love
Summertime sundog.

Captivating Limericks

Hate came looking for love.
Didn't believe in the heavens above.
So love removed a thin line.
Made hate kind of kind.
And showed hate what love was made of.

A man found an abundance of green.
The first money tree he'd ever seen.
But he didn't like money.
Until it stuck to him like honey.
And now he's a money fiend.

Acknowledgements

Shannon Woodard - Calvert Library and the libraries of Southern Maryland, commendable state of the art libraries.

City of New Orleans and the Saints for their championship and fairytale end.

Mumbai, India (Bollywood), for their wonderful culture and sensational movie and films.

University of Oregon, for their never say die attitude and feats. Go Ducks, go Quack attack.

Barack Obama, President of the United States of America, changing the world for the better.

-Heroes of outstanding achievements-